Miyah Takes Action

Written by:
Rosalyn Collins

Miyah Takes Action by Rosalyn Collins

Published by Denotion Research Group

Copyright © 2022 Rosalyn Collins

ISBN: 978-1-958634-10-3

Printed in United States

1st Edition

Dedication

To *Tommy*, *Amani*, *Amiyah*, *Ahmari* and *Ahkeem*

Hello, I am Miyah Cross.
Today, I will show my classmates the TAKE ACTION badge!

I like to start my day with the TAKE ACTION creed:

My actions are selfless.
I will help those in need.
If I see something, I will not fear.
Taking action is my good deed.

At the bus stop, my friends are already waiting.
Suddenly, I see something...

Mari, your shoes are untied.

I would hate to see you trip.

I will hold your water bottle if you would like to fix it.

I quickly take a seat at the front of the bus.
Then, I see something...

11

We laugh the entire ride to school.

14

While standing outside at school, I hear loud, popping noises in the distance.

Next, I see something...

I ask Tommy how he is feeling to see if he is OK.
His family was in an accident just the other day!

We take the time to catch up a little and arrive at the classroom right before the bell rang.

Just as I was getting comfortable in class, Miss Robinson said, "POP QUIZ"!

Shortly after, I see something...

19

I have extra sheets of paper and a pencil, Jaxon. Good luck on the quiz!

21

I think I may have aced the quiz!

Following the quiz, we walk to the cafeteria for lunch.

We eat until there is nothing left to eat.

On the way back from the cafeteria, I hear kids talking loudly. After that, I see something...

30

Keemi, thanks for putting me on game.

I was able to get a couple pairs for the price of one pair of the other brand.

And these shoes are definitely more stylish!

Upon return to the class, Miss Robinson announced that it is finally time for *Show* and *Tell*.

Guess who gets to go first!

I am so excited to show the class my TAKE ACTION badge.

34

This badge reminds us to
- be helpful when we can
- lift others up
- challenge norms
- be the best version of ourselves, even when others are not

35

Take Action

If we see something that does not seem right or fair, we cannot be afraid to do something.

See something,
Do something

Above all, this badge encourages us to do something when it could matter most. Whether a big or small act, we will never fully know our impact.

I am proud to present this charge to TAKE ACTION to you.

[Your name here]

Takes Action!

The End